Manufacturer: First published in Great Britain in 2025 by Buster Books, an imprint of
Michael O'Mara Books Limited, 9 Lion Yard, Tremadoc Road, London SW4 7NQ
www.mombooks.com

Represented by: Authorised Rep Compliance Ltd, Ground Floor,
71 Lower Baggot Street, Dublin D02 P593, Ireland
www.arccompliance.com

 www.mombooks.com/buster

 Buster Books

 @buster_books

A CIP catalogue record for this book is available from the British Library.

ISBN: 978-1-78055-941-4

3 5 7 9 10 8 6 4 2

This product is made of material from well-managed, FSC®-certified
forests and other controlled sources. The manufacturing processes
conform to the environmental regulations of the country of origin.

Printed and bound in May 2025 by
CPI Group (UK) Ltd, Croydon, CR0 4YY

	MIX
FSC	Paper | Supporting responsible forestry
www.fsc.org	FSC® C013604

For further information see www.mombooks.com/about/sustainability-climate-focus
Report any safety issues to product.safety@mombooks.com

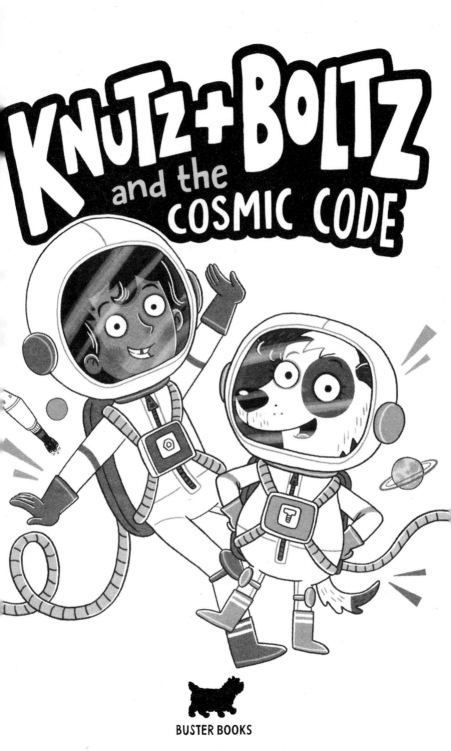

KNUTZ + BOLTZ
and the
COSMIC CODE

BUSTER BOOKS

Written by
Tim Collins

Illustrated by
Louise Forshaw

With special thanks to Ludovic Sallé

Edited by Frances Evans
Designed by Zoe Bradley and Jack Clucas
Cover design by John Bigwood
Consultancy by Damara Strong

CONTENTS

INTRODUCTION:
MEET KNUTZ AND BOLTZ

Hello! My name is Knutz and this is my best friend and super-scientist, Boltz.

You forgot 'inventor of the world's first self-fetching stick'!

Boltz and I are inventors and we love all things to do with Science, Technology, Engineering, Art and Maths – or STEAM for short. Are you ready to join us on a puzzle-filled, action-packed adventure?

CHAPTER ONE:
Lift-Off!

The time had come. We were actually going into **space**. It had all happened so fast, and we'd been so busy training, that it hadn't really sunk in.

The guard drove the buggy up to the launch pad, and I stepped out. I hoped she couldn't see how much I was quaking inside my spacesuit.

My dog, Boltz, leapt out after me. She didn't seem nervous at all. Her tail was wagging, and she looked more like she was about to fetch a tennis ball than embark upon a dangerous **secret mission**.

"You two have a great journey," said the guard.

"We will," said Boltz. "See you when we return."

The guard drove away, smiling and waving.

"She wouldn't look so cheery if she knew what we were going into space for," I said.

"Quiet, Knutz!" hissed Boltz. "Someone might overhear."

I looked around us. There were still a few engineers walking around the huge metal frame that supported the rocket. It didn't look like they were close enough to hear, but I supposed we couldn't take any chances.

Our mission was so top-secret that the only others who knew about it were the World Space Agency and the three other astronauts waiting for us in the space station.

That's because the truth would have been too much for everyone to bear.

We were going into space to **save Earth**. An asteroid was heading directly for the planet, and it was going to wipe out all life. The heads of the World Space Agency had come up with a plan to knock it off course, and they'd chosen us for the mission.

If everyone on Earth knew the danger they were in, the world would descend into **chaos**. Humans would scream, dogs would bark, cats would destroy sofas, and there would be panic in the streets. They couldn't know about their peril, for their own sakes.

We stepped into the elevator at the bottom of the metal frame, and Boltz pressed the button with 'crew' marked on it. This would take us to the section at the top of the rocket containing *Spacecraft 2*, which we would fly to the World Space Station.

We rose up through the frame, passing the three stages of the rocket, before reaching the top level.

The elevator stopped and Boltz dragged the metal door aside. She got out and strolled down the gangway to the crew hatch. For a moment, I couldn't force myself to move. The thought of blasting into space had drained all the strength from my body.

"Maybe we should ask them to put the journey off," I said. "The other astronauts might sort everything out without us."

"Too late," said Boltz.

She pointed down to the ground far below, where the last of the engineers were leaving the metal frame. They looked like **tiny specks** from so high up. My stomach flipped as I realized that soon entire cities would look like tiny specks as we circled around the Earth.

"Besides, I don't want the others to have all the fun of saving the planet without us."

Boltz was right. I'd achieved plenty of things in my life as a scientist and inventor already. But everything, even my one-hundred-metre swimming certificate, would pale in comparison to **rescuing** Earth.

I followed Boltz down the gangway on trembling legs.

Looks like it's time to go! We just need to program the ship's computer by telling it the order the following stages of lift-off go in. Can you help us put them in the right order and match each stage to the correct image on the opposite page?

A.
The flames, hot gases and smoke push down towards the ground, lifting the rocket off the launch pad and propelling it upwards.

B.
The main stages of the rocket fall away, leaving the spacecraft orbiting Earth.

C.
Fuel starts to burn in the rocket's engines.

D.
The rocket travels at a high speed, producing enough thrust to escape Earth's gravity.

E.
Flames, hot gases and smoke stream out of the exhaust nozzles of the rocket.

Answer on p230

Boltz typed the numbers into *Spacecraft 2*'s computer, and a 'System ready' message flashed on the screen.

The countdown from mission control boomed out through the speakers

"Ten ... nine ... eight ... seven ... six ..."

I tried to make myself smile, knowing that all the World Space Agency staff would be staring at my face on their screens.

"Five ... four ... three ... two ... one ..."

A series of loud clangs rang out as the metal frame detached itself, then there was a **huge explosion** of fuel beneath us.

I clung to my chair as we hurtled upwards. It felt like a giant hand was pressing me down into my seat.

Words and numbers raced across the screen in front of me, but the rocket was shaking around too much for me to read them. The mission-control chief was saying something over the speakers, but I was too busy trying to stop myself from whimpering to listen.

My smile had turned into frozen grimace, and there were tears streaming out of the corners of my eyes.

I turned to Boltz, who was grinning.

"I feel pretty emotional, too," she said. "Who'd have thought we'd make it all the way into space one day? I can't wait to tell the dogs in the park about this when we're back."

I didn't want to admit that I was crying with fear rather than wonder.

There was a mighty wrench, followed by another, and then another.

"We're breaking apart!" I cried. "It's all going **wrong**!"

"Of course we're breaking apart," said Boltz. "That's what rockets do when they've left Earth's atmosphere, remember?"

We'd gone through it over and over again in training, but I'd forgotten it all in my panic. We didn't need the rocket now we were high above Earth. It had released our space capsule, and now it was falling down into the ocean.

The imaginary hand that had been pushing me into my seat went away, and I was floating, held down only by the straps.

The mission-control commander came in over the speaker:

"Congratulations on a successful take-off!"

We need to turn the front of the spacecraft
so we're facing the right way to dock
with the space station.

Every time I press the black button,
we'll turn 20 degrees clockwise.

Every time I press the grey button,
we'll turn 20 degrees anticlockwise.

How many times will I have to press the black
button until we're facing the right way? Use the
protractor to help you reach an answer.

WSA 001

WSA 002

Answer on p230

We approached the space station ...

Docked ...

20

There were five astronauts waiting for us in the docking bay. We'd been expecting to meet Mei from China, Amir from India, and Brandon from the USA, but no one had told us about the other two.

There was a girl and a cat, who looked about the same age as us.

"Hi," said the girl. "I'm Venus."

"I'm Knutz," I said. I tried to walk towards her and shake her hand, but I found myself **floating** upwards. I'd been warned that moving around in the space station would be very different, but it was still quite a surprise.

The cat held his paw out to Boltz.

"I'm Mars," he said. "You might know me as the inventor of the automatic scratching post."

Boltz doesn't like cats much, and I was worried that she might growl at him, but she took his paw and shook it.

"I'm Boltz," she said. "You might know me as the inventor of the bark-activated vacuum cleaner."

"Come to the **command room**," said Mei. "We'll talk you through everything."

Mei, Amir and Brandon pulled themselves down the corridor by grabbing the handrails on the walls, and we followed.

The others were clearly used to getting about in space, but I kept finding my feet rising up, and getting confused about what was the ceiling and what was the floor.

Venus turned back to me.

"They didn't tell us that you and your dog were coming. They told us we'd been chosen because we were the best young scientists in the world. Nobody mentioned any back-ups."

Mei looked over her shoulder at us.

"You were the last four in our search," she said. "You all **really impressed** us and we couldn't decide, so Brandon suggested inviting all of you."

"But never mind **why** you were chosen," said Amir. "We need to focus on **what** you've been chosen to do. We don't have much time."

Knutz and Boltz obviously don't understand what's happening here, so I might as well try to explain.

We're not in ZERO GRAVITY on the space station, we're in FREEFALL. It's not the same thing.

We're orbiting around Earth. This means that Earth's gravity is acting on us and we're constantly falling towards the planet. But because we're travelling so fast, we never actually hit Earth. We just go around it in a circle.

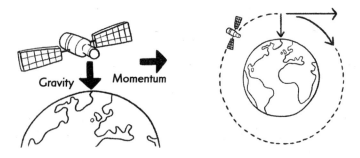

Gravity   Momentum

The reason we float is because we're falling all the time.

We go around Earth once every 90 minutes. I bet Knutz and Boltz can't even work out how many times a day that is ... Can you help them?

1. Can you work out how many times the space station goes around Earth every 12 hours?

2. And how many times does the space station go around Earth every 24 hours?

27

Answer on p231

I finally managed to strap myself into my workstation. Brandon pointed to a large screen, which was showing an image of Earth.

"As you all know, the planet is facing its greatest threat since the extinction of the dinosaurs," he said.

"And we're going to save it," said Mars. He held his paw up to Venus and they high-fived. Well, she high-fived. I suppose he high-foured, technically.

"You're right," said Brandon. "We **are** going to save it. And we'll all be remembered as heroes. But it's going to be tough, and we'll need to be at our **absolute best**. So, listen carefully, focus, and wait until after we're done to celebrate."

Venus and Mars switched their grins into serious expressions.

Brandon touched the screen and an image of a drone with a laser gun on the top appeared.

"Meet the USCC," he said. "Our chief weapon in the fight against the asteroid. It stands for 'Unmanned Space Combat Craft'."

"Or unwomaned," said Venus.

"Or uncatted," said Mars.

"Or undogged," said Boltz.

Brandon swept his hand across the screen and the image of the drone spun round.

"It's something we've been working on for years," he said. "Though we hoped we'd never need it. Every USCC unit carries a powerful laser, and we'll be using these lasers to hit the asteroid and change its course, so it **misses Earth**."

Brandon turned back to us.

"There are seven drones in total, one for each of us," he said. "We'll use the joysticks to steer them and the red buttons to fire the lasers."

He tapped the screen again, and a timer appeared:

"We have just over four hours until the asteroid enters **firing range**," he said. "I've created a program that simulates the route we'll take, and we're going to practise it until we know it backwards."

Venus stuck her hand up.

"Excuse me," she said. "What is the probability of each drone hitting the asteroid?"

"Thirty-three per cent," said Brandon.

Probability is the part of maths that looks at the chances of something happening.

Probabilities can be written as percentages, where 100% means something definitely *will* happen, and 0% means something definitely *won't* happen.

If there's a 75% chance that something will happen, it means there's a 25% chance it won't. And a 50% chance that something will happen means there's a 50% chance that it won't. In each case, the numbers add up to 100.

33% is roughly the same as a one in three chance. For example, if you roll a dice, there's a one in three chance that you'll roll a 1 or a 2.

1. What is the probability that you won't roll a 1 or a 2?

2. Using Mars' calculations, what is the probability that the mission WON'T succeed?

Answer on p231

But don't worry; it won't come to that. The drones won't fail.

CHAPTER TWO:
The Asteroid Approaches

Brandon jabbed the large screen and an animation of the asteroid hitting Earth played. When it struck, a huge cloud of dust swept over the planet.

If we failed the mission, we wouldn't have anywhere to go back to. The only people or animals who could survive would be the ones rich enough to live in the space hotels owned by the billionaire Brad Piper. Everyone else would perish.

Now Brandon played an animation of the USCC drones flying up to the asteroid. The first drone fired a laser into the asteroid and altered its path. Earth was safe.

"That's all we need," said Mei. "Just one hit from seven attempts."

Brandon touched the screen again, and it showed a diagram of the seven drones.

"Each USCC drone has enough energy to shoot its high-powered laser for **ten seconds**," he said. "You'll all need to get into position and be ready to fire. But you'll only have to do it if the other drones have missed. I'll go first, and I fully expect it to be all over after my turn."

He swiped the screen again, and we could see the view of space from one of the drone's cameras. There was a line of small green triangles showing the path ahead.

"These markers will guide your way," he said, "both in the simulation, and when we do it for real. But don't rely on them. Get to know your route, so you can feel confident."

We use sets of letters and numbers, known as 'co-ordinates', to find things on grids. We write them in brackets with the number or letter on the horizontal axis (x-axis) written first, and the number or letter on the vertical axis (y-axis) written second.

For example, in this grid, the planet is sitting in (D, 4):

Brandon's drone is located at (L, 14). What are the co-ordinates of the six other drones?

y

4
3
2
1
0
9
8
7
6
5
4
3
2
1

A B C D E F G H I J K L M N

x

37

Answer on p232

We'll be last. That means it will all be down to us if the others miss!

Were you even listening? He just said you'll go after us. We won't miss. You really might as well not be here.

I ignored Venus's taunts and looked at the drone simulation on my laptop.

We had to steer, speed up and slow down using our joysticks, and fire with the red buttons next to them. I struggled at first, but soon managed to get the hang of it. I even started enjoying it, and felt like I was playing a computer game. But then I had to remind myself how serious it was. It would be game over for the **whole world** if we got it wrong.

I noticed that Boltz was panting as she gazed at her screen, and I realized I was thirsty, too. We hadn't had anything to drink since we'd been back on Earth.

It would be easy to forget about eating and drinking on the space station. My senses of taste and smell were much weaker, and it was hard to keep track of time.

I leaned over to Venus and Mars.

"Do you know where we can get a bottle of water from?"

They both burst out laughing.

"A bottle?" asked Mars. "We're in freefall, remember? Have you any idea what would happen if you opened a bottle?"

I cringed at my stupid mistake. In training, they'd explained to us that liquid would float around in the air up here. The only way to drink things was through a straw in a sealed pouch.

"He meant a pouch," said Boltz. "There's no need to be so rude."

"I think my friend was just a little surprised," said Venus. "This trip is meant to be for **elite scientists** only."

"We're all under a lot of pressure," I said. "We should be helping each other."

Mars unstrapped himself from his workstation.

"Okay," he said. "I'll help you by fetching the water. IF you can tell me its **chemical formula**."

Well, that's easy! An element is a substance made from only one type of atom. Elements can't be broken down into other substances.

Hydrogen (H) and oxygen (O) are important elements that make up most of what we see around us.

Hydrogen is the most abundant element in the universe, while humans and other living creatures depend on oxygen to breathe and live.

Chemical formulas are used when atoms become bonded together. The chemical formula for water is H_2O. This means two atoms of hydrogen bonded to one atom of oxygen.

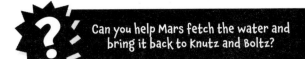

Can you help Mars fetch the water and bring it back to Knutz and Boltz?

START

FINISH

Answer on p232

I watched in horror as the blobs of water floated around the control room.

Mei, Amir and Brandon looked up from their workstations and scowled.

"Clean that up!" yelled Amir. "Quickly!"

I looked around for a mop, before realizing it wouldn't be any use. The only way I could get rid of the water would be to swoop around and **gobble** it up.

I unhooked myself from my workstation and flapped around like a panicking chicken. A blob was heading for Mei's face, so I lunged forwards to swallow it, but accidentally elbowed her in the cheek.

"Watch out!" she said.

"Sorry!" I cried.

Another blob was heading for the giant screen, so I clawed at the wall and pulled myself over to it, managing to kick Brandon in the back of the head.

"Whoops!" I yelled.

"Careful!" he cried.

I gulped the water down, trying to forget what Mars had said about it being **recycled wee**.

A few more blobs were down near the floor, so I spun upside down to get them. My shoes must have caught a cable on the ceiling, because the giant screen went **blank**.

"Look where you're going!" shouted Amir.

He unhooked himself and drifted up to fix the screen.

I pulled myself along the floor, gulping down the last blobs.

"It's not his fault," said Boltz. "Mars told us our water pouches were recycled wee. Knutz fell for the prank and spat it out in surprise."

I was expecting Mars to deny it, but he just grinned.

"I admit it, I did say that."

Amir plugged the cable back in and the screen came on. He looked down at Boltz.

"Of course we drink recycled wee," he said. "We wouldn't be able to **survive** if we didn't."

We couldn't live on this station if we didn't recycle water.
That's why we invented this water recovery system:

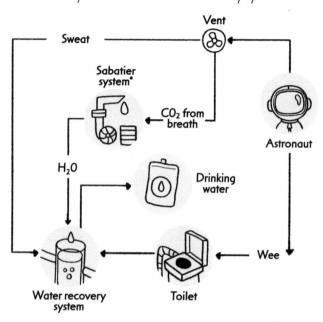

It runs urine through a special processor that turns it into clean water.
The system also processes water from breath and sweat, which is
collected from the air. This might sound gross, but it really isn't!
The machine works so well that the water is cleaner than
anything you'd get out of a tap on Earth.

48

*A reactor that helps reduce carbon
dioxide and produce water.

Each astronaut needs 3 litres of drinking water per day. How much drinking water will all 7 astronauts need per day? Can you gather the fewest number of water pouches required for the astronauts?

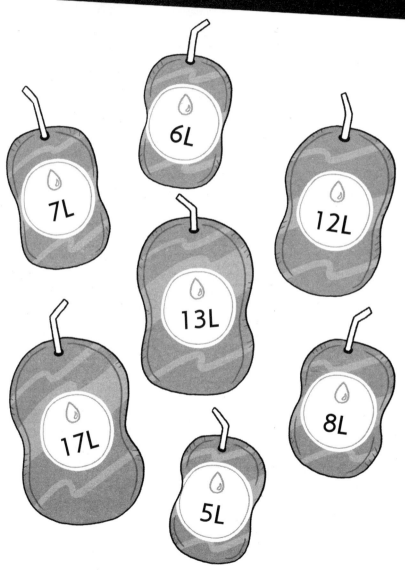

Answer on p233

We'd been shown a diagram of the station in training, so I thought I'd have no problem getting about it. But being there was different. I kept turning around as I pulled myself along on the hand rails, and losing track of what was the floor and what was the ceiling.

We passed a round white door with 'AIRLOCK' written on it.

"I hope we get to go through there and see the outside of the station," said Boltz.

"I hope we don't," I said. "Astronauts only use it in **emergencies**."

We continued into a corridor with sleeping pods along the walls. These were the space station version of bedrooms. They were small booths, just big enough for a human or animal to fit inside, with padded sleeping bags fixed to the walls.

"They look quite cosy," said Boltz. "Like high-tech dog baskets. It's just a shame we'll be too busy to use them."

"I'm sure we can have a nap once we've saved the world," I said. "Anyone would deserve a rest after that."

The toilet was at the end of this corridor, and we'd been told all about it at space camp. There was a small bowl for pooing in, and a nozzle for weeing in. I'd have to make sure I did it just right when the time came. It had been bad enough following blobs of water around, and it would be a million times more embarrassing chasing wee.

We carried along until we came to the **kitchen**, which was a long room with hundreds of clear bags stuck to the walls. Inside were small sealed pouches of food that had been specially treated to last a long time.

"Whoever stocked these pouches had great taste," said Boltz.

She pulled out a pouch of salmon-flavoured dog biscuits and tossed some into the air. Then she swooped around and snapped them into her mouth.

I wished I could be as excited about the human options, but they all looked very **dry** and **tasteless**.

Here are the meals of each astronaut. Can you use the key to work out which meal weighs the most?

KEY:

Tortilla
70g

Cracker
10g

Peanuts
12g

Dog biscuit
5g

Cat biscuit
4g

Chicken
60g

Sausage
50g

Cookie
20g

Apple
15g

Spinach
8g

Boltz

Mars

54

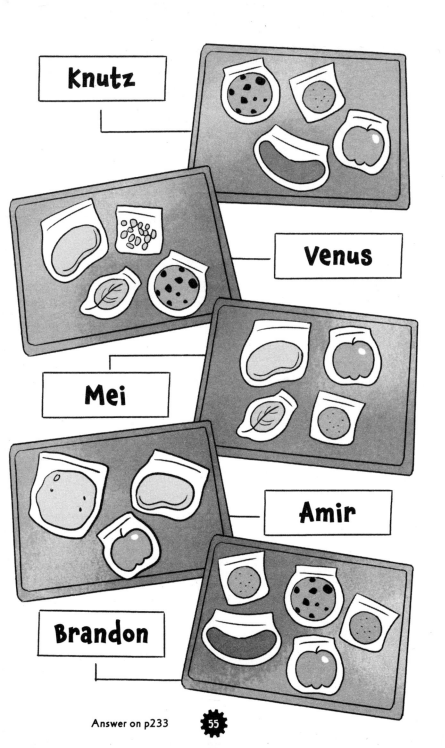

Knutz

Venus

Mei

Amir

Brandon

Answer on p233

Amir got out of his workstation and unclipped a length of thick black wire from one of the walls.

"Replace the damaged wire with this one," he said. "I'll shut down the solar array on the left of the ship while you do it."

We followed him out of the control room and over to the **airlock** we'd seen earlier. He pulled the round door open and pointed at a small cylindrical capsule behind it.

"Get inside and close the door," he said, handing the wire to Boltz. "After a few seconds, you'll be able to leave the outer door."

There were laptops on either side of the airlock, and their screens showed an overhead view of the **solar panels** and the two long metal arms that were next to them.

"The best way to move around outside is to fix the back of your suit to the inspection arm," said Amir, tapping on the keyboard of the first laptop.

"I'll control it with this computer and get you over to the damaged panel."

58

I'd seen one of these metal arms in the training camp a few days earlier, and I was sure I could work it.

"Please can I control it?" I asked. "I know how it works."

Amir **squinted** at me. No doubt he was remembering the unfortunate incident with the water.

"I promise I won't mess things up this time."

"All right," he said, and pulled himself back along the corridor. "Let us know as soon as you're done so I can get the power back on."

Boltz fixed her helmet on and stepped into the airlock. She closed the door behind her and I turned to the laptop screen. A minute later, I saw her leave the airlock, close the outer door behind her and clip the metal arm to a hook on the back of her suit.

She turned to the camera and stuck her paw up, and I tapped the keyboard to move her forwards.

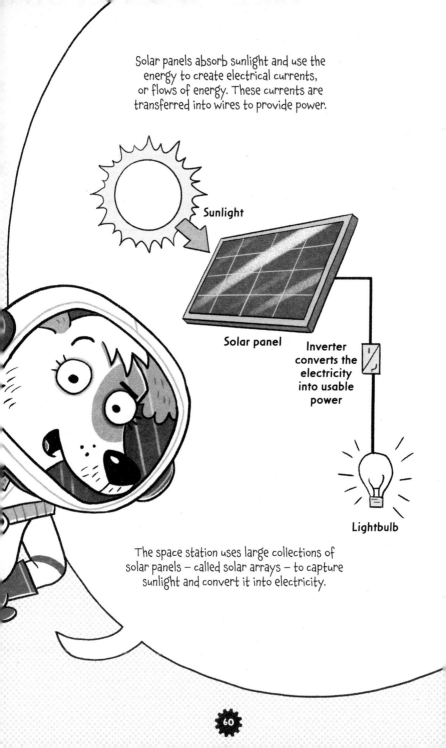

Solar panels absorb sunlight and use the energy to create electrical currents, or flows of energy. These currents are transferred into wires to provide power.

Sunlight

Solar panel

Inverter converts the electricity into usable power

Lightbulb

The space station uses large collections of solar panels — called solar arrays — to capture sunlight and convert it into electricity.

Can you use the directions given below to guide Boltz to the faulty wire on the solar array? From the grid square marked 'START', follow each direction (up, down, left or right) by that number of squares. For example, 'U2' means you go up 2 squares. The panel that you end up at is the one with the faulty wire. Directions: R3, D5, R4, U2, R1, U2, L2, D3, L4

START For Boltz →

START For Mars

I don't trust Boltz to sort this out on her own. Guide me to the faulty panel, too. Directions: R4, U1, R5, U6, L4, D3, L3, D1

Answer on p234

I was so focused on controlling the arm that I hadn't seen Mars getting into the airlock. I only noticed him when he appeared on the screen, clipping himself to the other metal arm.

It swooped out towards the damaged panel, and I looked right and saw that Venus was controlling it from the other laptop.

"Stop that!" I said. "Amir gave US permission to fix the panel, not YOU."

"This is too important to leave to **amateurs**," said Venus.

She tapped at her keyboard, moving Mars right next to Boltz.

"Let Boltz do it on her own," I said. "She knows how to fix it. She's one of the best young scientists on the planet."

"So I've been told," said Venus. "Though I haven't seen much evidence so far. My science teacher would probably move her down to the puppy class."

I watched the screen **in horror** as Boltz and Mars fought over the wire, and it spun away into space.

"Now look what's happened!" I said.

"It's your dog's fault. She should have let Mars help."

We guided the arms back down to the airlock and let Boltz and Mars back in. I was worried Boltz would get angry and try to bite Mars, but she just growled under her breath.

Amir looked at us in confusion when we returned to the control room.

"The system is still showing damage," he said. "What happened?"

"The little doggie **messed up**," said Venus. "I've no idea why you trusted her with something so important."

"Only because that cat interfered!" yapped Boltz.

Amir bolted out of his workstation.

"I don't want to hear it," he said. He dragged himself over to the wall, and unclipped another wire. "I knew I should have done it myself."

Mei pointed at our workstations.

"Strap yourselves back in, folks. The mission will begin soon."

I fixed myself into my workstation and wondered how much time had passed since we'd got on board.

Earth below us was constantly switching from light to dark, and I'd totally lost track.

Astronauts join the space station from many different time zones. To avoid confusion, they set their watches to Co-ordinated Universal Time, or UTC.

Our rocket set off from a space camp in the USA at 2 o'clock in the afternoon, or 14:00 on a 24-hour clock. We were in a time zone that was 5 hours behind UTC.

1. What time did we set off in UTC?

Answer on p234

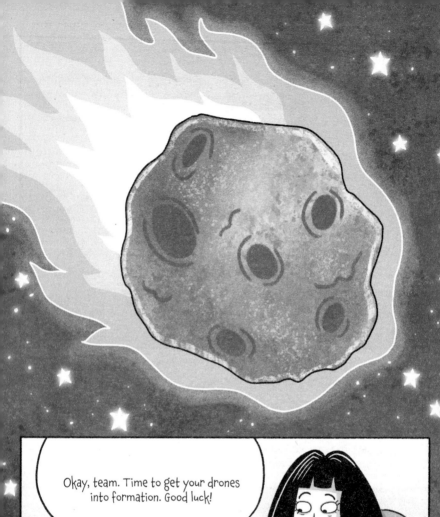

Okay, team. Time to get your drones into formation. Good luck!

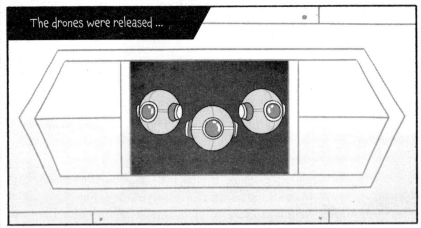

The drones were released ...

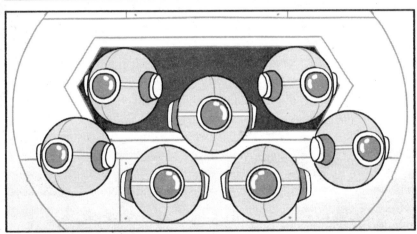

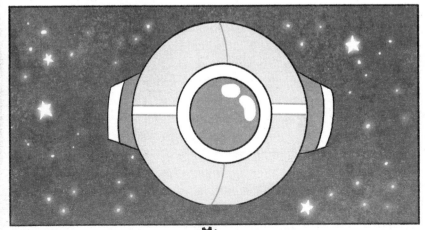

CHAPTER THREE:
Laser Attack!

My laptop screen showed me the view from my drone. The six others were ahead of me, and I followed them deep into space.

This part of the mission was easy. I just needed to rotate the drone by steering the joystick left or right, speed it up by pushing forwards, and slow it down by pulling back.

Brandon went in front, and the rest of us went after. It didn't feel too different from practising with the simulator, and I kept having to remind myself it was for **real** this time.

"Great work, team," said Brandon. "All good so far."

Brandon was looking back and forth from his laptop to the big screen, which showed the position of the drones.

"Assume attack formation ... **now**!" he said.

At this point in the simulation, the guiding triangles usually appeared on the screen. Brandon had said they'd be here now, but there was no sign of them.

My hands **trembled**, and I worried this would make the drone quake, too.

"What's happened?" asked Mei. "Where's the guidance system?"

Brandon frantically tapped at his keyboard.

"It's malfunctioning. Just guide your drones as well as you can. Can we do anything, Amir?"

My heart pounded. Even though we'd been through it many times, I wasn't sure I could do it without the arrows.

"The computer's code needs changing. Let me just try something ..."

"Don't!" said Brandon. "There isn't time."

Amir ignored him and tapped **frantically** on his keyboard.

Guiding triangles appeared on our screens, but there were far too many of them. Instead of just one path, there were three options, and I had no idea which one to pick.

"I told you!" shouted Brandon.

"It's okay," said Amir. "The triangles can still help us if we follow the right ones."

Equilateral triangles have three equal sides.

Isosceles triangles have two equal sides.

Scalene triangles have no equal sides.

The correct route is the one that only has equilateral and isosceles triangles. The others have scalene triangles, too.

Using this information, can you work out which is the correct route?

A.

B. C.

Answer on p235

75

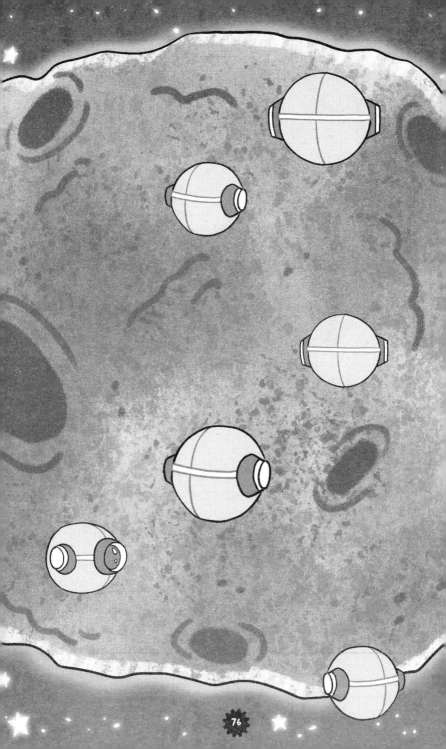

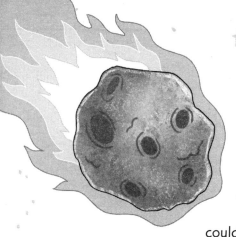

"There must be a fault with that drone," said Mei. "Move aside and I'll blast it."

On the big screen, I could see Brandon's drone dropping away. Mei's drone shot up to the asteroid. She pressed the red button.

"Nothing's happening!" she yelled.

Amir's drone flew up next. He jabbed at his button when he was in position, but again, it **didn't work**.

"The same thing's happening with mine!" he said. "Something's gone wrong with the laser guns."

"Can we bring the remaining ones back and try to fix them?" asked Mei.

Brandon shook his head.

"There's no time," he said. "Let's just carry on with the plan. One of them is bound to do it."

Mars flew his drone up next.

"None of you were pushing hard enough," he said. "You should have done it like this."

He jammed his finger down on the button, but still no laser appeared.

"Don't worry," said Venus. "Mine will work."

She guided her drone up and pressed the button. Yet again, nothing happened.

Boltz tried her best, but hers didn't work either.

There was just me left. Everyone else had failed, but if I could get mine to work, Earth would still be safe.

The others turned to look at me, and I did my best to look **confident**.

I waited until the drone was facing the asteroid and pressed the button.

Mine didn't fire either.

"Fly right into it!" shouted Amir. "It might still be enough to change its course!"

I pushed the joystick forwards. The giant rock got larger and **larger**, then my screen went dark.

Brandon stared at his laptop and shook his head.

"Good try, Knutz," said Brandon. "But it hasn't worked."

"Get the programming code for the drones up on the screen," said Mei. "We need to work out what went wrong."

Block code is a method of coding that uses jigsaw-like pieces. Each piece contains a pre-programmed instruction.

Users can drag and drop different pieces of code together to build computer programs, such as animations, games or, in our case, instructions for the drones.

Take a look at the code on the right – this is the one used for the drones. It looks as though a line has been changed.

Which line of code has been altered?

If joystick pressed right then
turn ⟶ 15 degrees

If joystick pressed left then
turn ⟵ 15 degrees

If red button pressed then
fire laser for 0 seconds

If joystick pressed forwards then
add 50 km per hour

If joystick pressed down then
minus 50 km per hour

Answer on p236

Amir climbed inside the spacecraft, tapped on the keyboard and a diagram of the missile appeared. A small cylindrical shape was flashing red in the middle of it.

"One of the fuel pumps is **missing**," said Amir. "We'll have to switch to *Spacecraft 2*."

Amir got out of the first spacecraft and pulled himself over to the one we'd arrived in. The same diagram with the same flashing red shape appeared.

"This one as well," he said.

"It makes no sense," said Mei. "Both spacecraft should have been checked at the space centre before they took off."

I thought back to our journey from Earth. There were plenty of engineers climbing the scaffolding as we approached the rocket. Could one of them have **sabotaged** it? But why would anyone want to do that? It would only make it more likely that Earth would be destroyed.

"How long will it take you to fix?" asked Mei.

"I'm not sure I can," said Amir. "We don't keep spare parts for missiles in the station."

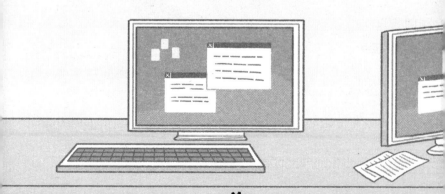

I pulled myself closer and looked at the diagram. There were two fuel pumps inside each missile, and one was missing from each.

"Why don't we take the fuel pump from the first spacecraft and use it in this one?" I asked.

Amir shook his head.

"The missiles need two different parts," he said. "A left pump and a right one. All we have is two left ones."

Mars sniggered and shook his head at me, as if this should have been obvious to everyone.

"We'll just have to try and use them anyway," said Brandon.

"There's no point," said Mei. "The missile won't fire at all without two working fuel pumps."

"Excuse me," said Venus. "You have a **3D printer** in the control room. Why don't you just use that to create a new part?"

Amir stared at her for a moment.

"Yes," he said. "That might just work."

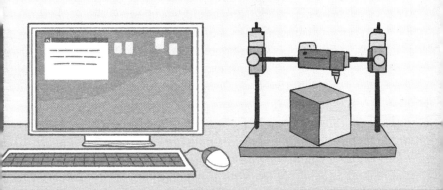

3D printers are machines that build objects one layer at a time. Many 3D printers use plastic, but ours can make things in metal. We use a computer-aided design (CAD) program to create the models to send to the printer.

3D printer

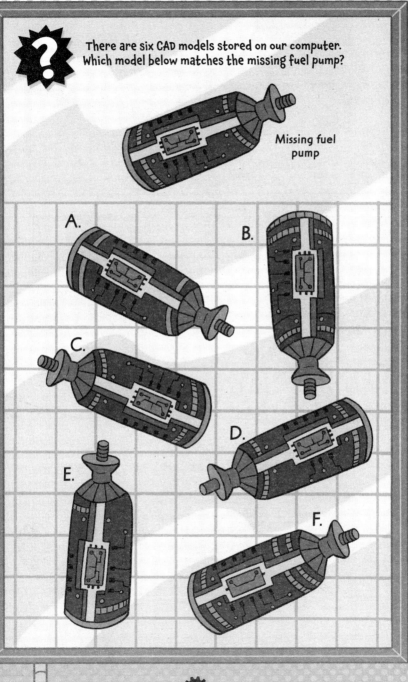

There are six CAD models stored on our computer. Which model below matches the missing fuel pump?

Missing fuel pump

A.

B.

C.

D.

E.

F.

Answer on p236

Perfect fit!

Back inside, Amir checked the computer screen ...

"It's ready to go," said Amir. He looked over at Brandon. "Can you program the course before I set off?"

"No need to," said Brandon. "I can pilot it remotely using the station's computer. All you'll have to do is fire the missile."

Amir strapped himself in.

"Stop," said Mei. "We'll need you here. It will be better to send one of the others."

She looked back at Boltz and I, then at Venus and Mars. I was prepared to take the challenge if chosen, but was secretly hoping she'd pick one of the others. Flying directly towards an asteroid didn't sound like the most relaxing day trip in the universe.

"I'll do it. Using the 3D printer was my idea, so it's only right that I should go."

"If Venus goes, I'm going too," said Mars.

"All right," said Mei.

Amir pulled himself out of the spacecraft, while Venus and Mars moved towards it.

Boltz pushed herself in front of them, **blocking** their way.

"I think Knutz and I should go instead. We were chosen for this mission, too, and I think we should be given a chance to destroy the asteroid."

Venus planted her hands on her hips and drifted upwards slightly.

"You two?" she asked. "So far, you've disrupted the crew by spitting water everywhere, proved you have no knowledge of what freefall is and made a complete mess of fixing the solar panel."

"That was your fault," yapped Boltz. "We were doing perfectly well until you two ruined everything."

Mei sighed.

"We don't have time for this, guys," she said. "The world is in danger. Remember?"

She pointed to the spacecraft.

"Venus and Mars, get inside," she said. "Everyone else move away."

Boltz let out a **low growl** as she floated aside.

Oh, come on. You must know this. A prime number is a number greater than 1 that can only be divided by itself and 1.

So 2 is a prime number, because it can only be divided by 1 and 2. In fact, it's the only even prime number!

3 is a prime number too, but 4 is not because it can be divided by 1, 2 and 4.

 Which are the other prime numbers?

Answer on p236

We went back to the control room, where Mei, Amir and Brandon were getting into their workstations. The big screen was showing the view from *Spacecraft 1*'s camera. I guessed that the small dot in the middle of it was the asteroid.

There was a **countdown** on the screen, showing that Venus and Mars were less than thirty minutes away from the asteroid. I was sure they'd hit it, but I just wanted it all to be over. I wished I could fast-forward time until they'd done it.

Boltz folded her arms and let herself float upwards.

"It's so unfair that they get to destroy the asteroid," she said. "It should have been us."

"Never mind," I said. "As long as someone does it, that's the most important thing."

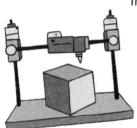

Boltz bobbed around the control room, looking at the bags of spare wires lining the walls. She stopped next to the 3D printer.

"Wait," she said. "We could get the other spacecraft ready while we're waiting for Venus and Mars to reach the asteroid. Then we'll have a **back-up** if something goes wrong."

I was sure we'd never have to use it, but I was glad to have something to do. Time seemed to be passing incredibly slowly.

Boltz dragged herself over to Brandon, who was staring at his screen.

"We want to print a **new fuel pump** and put it into the other missile," she said. "That way we can fly up to the asteroid if Venus and Mars fail."

"They won't fail," said Brandon. "So you don't need to."

Mei looked over at him.

"I don't see any harm in them getting it ready," she said.

Brandon turned to us and sighed.

"Fine, you can fix the other missile. But only if you can do it all on your own. We can't spare any time to help you."

I grabbed the replacement pump from the printer. Now for the hard bit. We had to fit it into the missile.

Boltz unclipped a drill from a toolbox on the wall, and we made our way down the corridor. She fixed her helmet on and entered the airlock. I went to the laptop on the left of the airlock, and watched as she emerged on the screen and hooked herself on to the **metal arm**.

It was much easier to control without Venus and Mars interfering, and I managed to guide Boltz over to the missile on the top of *Spacecraft 2* with no problem.

I watched as she opened the missile's casing, slotted the fuel pump in and drilled it all back together.

I was about to guide her back when she accidentally let go of the drill. It floated away and lodged itself between the spacecraft and the docking port.

"Leave it!" I cried into the microphone in my suit.

I watched in horror as Boltz **unclipped** the back of her suit and crawled along the top of the spacecraft towards the drill.

Boltz ignored me, and stretched her paw out to get the drill. She overreached, and slipped around the side of the spacecraft.

"There are plenty of other drills! It's not worth risking your life for!"

She grabbed a solar panel on the far side and clung to it.

I could hear her yapping into her microphone, and see her **wide eyes** through her helmet.

"Hold on!" I yelled.

My heart pounded as I looked around the corridor, trying to work out what to do. I was terrified that the strength in Boltz's arms would run out before I could think of anything, and she'd drift away into space.

I saw a bag with lengths of thick wire inside. Maybe I could go out, dangle one down to her and drag her back up. But then I might slip, too, and we'd both be lost.

It was no use. I'd have to go and interrupt the others.

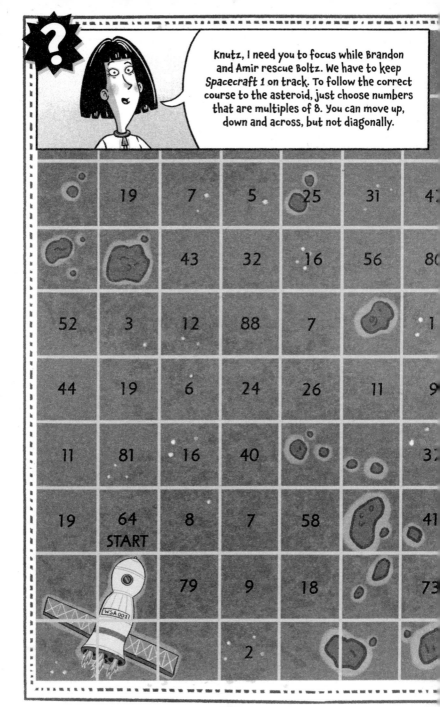

1	65	92	17			
9		26				
4	13					
4	8		88			
2	48	81	72	8		
6	24	34	50	48	74	13
1	32	56	80	16	25	74
0	14	9	15		4	21
3	2	39	54	12		
2	23	84	26	70	6	19

Answer on p236

I stared at the view from *Spacecraft 1* on the big screen and gripped the joystick. Steering it was easy enough. The difficult bit would be getting Venus and Mars close enough to the asteroid to fire the missile, and then ducking them safely out of the way. I hoped Brandon would be back by then.

I glanced over at Mei's laptop, which was showing the outside of the station. Amir was holding a long metal pole out to Boltz, who was grabbing the end.

Mei spotted me looking, so I turned my attention back to the main screen.

Brandon and Amir soon came back into the control room, followed by Boltz. She took her helmet off and tried to grin, but I could tell she was embarrassed. Her ears were drooping and her tail was tucked between her legs.

"What went wrong?" asked Mei.

"I think my costume unclipped itself from the metal arm," said Boltz. "It must be faulty."

I was about to tell the others the truth about how she'd tried to rescue the drill, but she glared at me and mimed a **zipping movement** across her lips.

"Everything seems to be malfunctioning at the moment," said Amir.

"Never mind about it now," said Brandon. I got out of the way so he could take over the controls again. "Venus and Mars are getting close."

Mei pressed a button on the top of her suit.

"Venus and Mars, can you hear us?" she asked.

"Loud and clear," said the voice of Venus from the speakers of the big screen.

"And we're ready to save Earth!" yelled Mars.

I found myself hoping they'd miss so they'd stop being **so smug**. But then I remembered that this would mean the end of the world, so it wouldn't really be worth it.

"Stand by for missile launch," said Brandon.

Venus and Mars need to fire the missile when they are exactly 80 km from the asteroid.

Which of the following options equals 80?

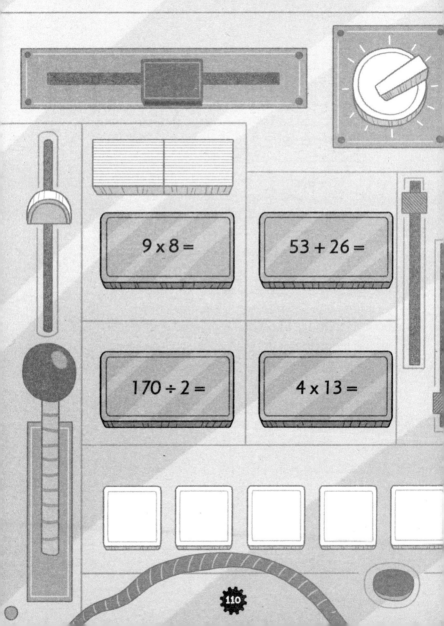

9 x 8 =

53 + 26 =

170 ÷ 2 =

4 x 13 =

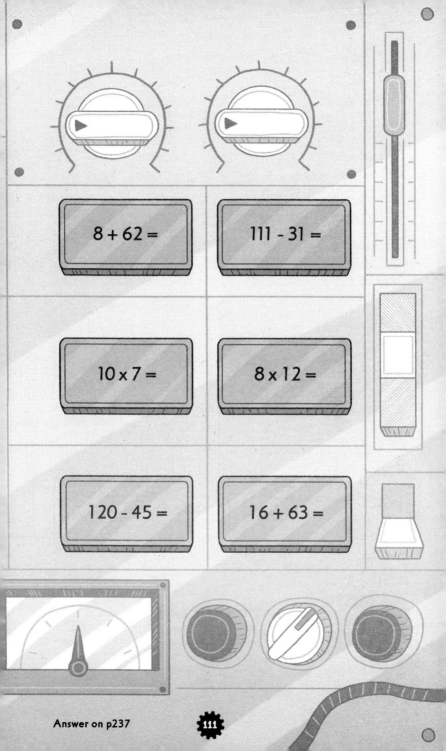

8 + 62 =

111 − 31 =

10 x 7 =

8 x 12 =

120 − 45 =

16 + 63 =

Answer on p237

111

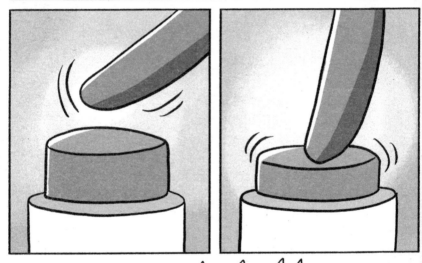

FIRE!

CHAPTER FOUR:
Last Chance

I couldn't believe what I was seeing. Venus and Mars
had **missed**. Their only job had been to fire the
missile at the right moment, and they'd failed.

My hands tensed into fists as I thought about how
they'd messed everything up. Boltz had been right,
after all. They should have chosen us.

Then it sunk in. This meant it was **our** turn now.
We'd have to fly up to the asteroid and destroy it.
And this time there could be no mistakes.

"What happened?" asked Mei.

"They must have mistimed their shot," said
Brandon. "Even getting it wrong by a **split second**
can make a difference."

Mei turned to us. She'd been calm and confident
up until this point, but now she was trembling.
A bead of sweat floated off her forehead.

Boltz lifted her paw to her head in a salute.

"We won't let you down," she said.

She hurried down the corridor with her tail wagging, propelling herself forwards by grabbing the walls. Brandon followed after her.

When I got to the docking bay, Brandon was inside the spacecraft and checking the computer.

"I told them they should have picked us first," said Boltz. "Of course Venus and Mars were going to get it wrong. They were probably too busy high-fiving each other to press the button."

"Never mind," I said. "At least we know we'll be able to do it."

Boltz stared at me for a moment. Her tail fell still.

"We certainly should be able to do it," she said. "But everything seems to have gone wrong with the mission so far. It's **odd**."

She looked back at the spacecraft.

"Well," she said. "All we can do is try our best."

Brandon got back out of the spacecraft.

"Strap yourselves in and transfer the controls so I can pilot you remotely," he said. "I'll soon have you on the way."

We pulled ourselves inside.

To switch the controls of *Spacecraft 2* to us, you need to use a code based on fractions.

Fractions tell you how many parts of a whole you have. They are written by placing one number above another, as with $\frac{1}{2}$. The top number is known as the 'numerator' and the bottom number is known as the 'denominator'. Some fractions have the same value. For example, $\frac{1}{2}$ is the same as $\frac{2}{4}$.

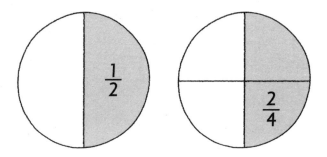

If you work out which of the fractions opposite have the same value, it will give you a code in the form A1 B2 C3 D4, which you can input into the computer.

What is the code you get if you match the fractions with the same value?

A) $\frac{2}{6}$

B) $\frac{10}{12}$

C) $\frac{3}{4}$

D) $\frac{1}{7}$

1) $\frac{6}{8}$

2) $\frac{1}{3}$

3) $\frac{2}{14}$

4) $\frac{5}{6}$

Answer on p238

"I don't care what you have to say," said Boltz. "You messed things up, and now we've got to take care of everything."

Venus leant forwards. Her eyes were wide and her smug grin was gone. Mars looked nervous, too. His fur was on end and his ears were pinned back.

"This is **serious**," said Venus. "We had to hack our spacecraft's computer so we could speak to you. Firstly, don't respond to anything we say. They can't hear Mars and me, but they can still see and hear you on the station."

"So what if they can?" asked Boltz.

"Shhh!" said Mars. "They mustn't hear you. There's a **traitor** in the crew!"

I expected Boltz to shout back at them. All the other astronauts had been helpful and friendly since we'd arrived at the station, while Venus and Mars had been nothing but rude. But, to my surprise, she stayed silent and sat back in her seat.

Mei's voice came through the ship's computer.

"Are you trying to say something, Boltz?" she asked. "We didn't understand your last message."

"No, we're good," I said, sticking my thumb up.

"And all set to save Earth," said Boltz.

Mei didn't reply, so I supposed this must have been convincing.

"Excellent," said Venus. "They aren't on to us yet, but I'll have to be quick. Try not to react to what I'm about to tell you, even if it makes you angry. The traitor is Brandon. He's been **sabotaging** the mission at every stage."

I wanted to gasp, but forced my mouth to stay closed.

Boltz let out a low growl.

"The first thing you need to do is record a loop of yourselves and broadcast it as the spacecraft's output," said Mars. "That way they won't be able to see or hear you. Do you know how to do that?"

Boltz nodded.

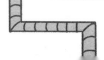

It's easy to create a video loop. I'll film us with the computer's camera for a few seconds, then I'll upload the footage into video-editing software, and program it to repeat over and over.

The only tricky thing is making sure the first frame matches the last exactly.

Which frame should we use as the last one?

First frame:

A.

B.

C.

D.

E.

F.

G.

Answer on p238

The asteroid was looming larger. Soon we'd be in **firing range**.

"You need to find a way to get the spacecraft back under your own control," said Venus.

Thoughts raced through my mind so quickly that I didn't know what to say.

"We'll work it out," said Boltz.

"Listen," said Mars. "We've got to go now, but I'm sorry if we've been rude to you. We didn't know another pair of young scientists were joining the mission."

"I'm sure it was all part of Brandon's plan to disrupt things," said Venus. "He wanted us to be so busy competing against each other that we wouldn't realize what he was up to. He was the one who told us to fix the solar panel at the same time as you. We should have refused."

I imagined Brandon's glee when he saw Boltz and Mars fighting on the station. He was probably hoping they'd both **drift off** into space.

"We're sorry, too," said Boltz. "But thanks for telling us the truth."

They disappeared from the screen and I could see Mei, Amir and Brandon again. None of them looked **suspicious**, so I guessed the video loop was working.

Boltz tapped the keyboard and a 'Switch to manual control' option appeared. She clicked on it and a picture of some planets appeared. There were blank text boxes next to each one.

"Looks like a security check," said Boltz. "I think we just have to name the planets."

I recognized the image straight away. The huge curve of the Sun was on the left, and the eight planets of our solar system were shown in order of their distance from it.

I should have known the exact order of the planets, but my panic was getting the better of me, and I could only remember a few scraps of information.

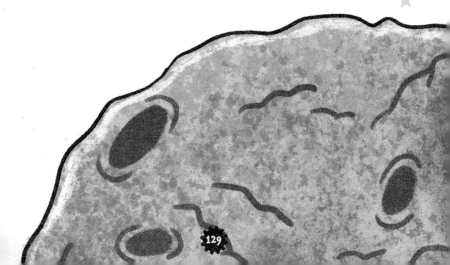

Answer on p239

"It will be much safer if you can give control back to us," said Mei. "We can't afford any mistakes."

"Don't worry!" said Boltz. "We can do this."

The asteroid was almost upon us. I could see its lumpy surface as we **hurtled** towards it.

"Fire!"

I pressed the red button.

I was expecting to feel a huge rumble above us and watch the missile shoot out, but nothing happened.

I pressed the button again. It still didn't work.

Boltz reached over and slammed her paw down on it, but there was still no effect.

"This must be Brandon's doing," she whispered. "When he pretended to be checking the computer, he was actually **disabling that button**."

All the strength drained out of my body. We'd put ourselves through so much to get here, and it was all for nothing.

"So that's it?" I asked. "We've failed?"

Boltz gazed at the approaching asteroid in silence for a second.

"Not quite," she said. "I think there's a way to save Earth. But we won't be able to save ourselves."

I quaked inside my suit. I knew what she was about to say, but I didn't want to hear it. The only way we could give Earth a chance would be to sacrifice ourselves.

"I can program the spacecraft to fly straight into the asteroid," she said. "It will hit it, the missile will explode and the asteroid will change course. But we'll be left floating in space without a ship."

I wanted to tell Boltz there was another way. That we could fly back to the station and work with Venus and Mars to come up with a new plan. But I knew it would be too late by then. This was the **only option**.

Billions of humans and animals would die if we selfishly put our own survival first. And what were the lives of one boy and one dog compared to all those others?

"Looks like we've got no choice," I said.

"Abandon spacecraft!"

Can you work out which group below matches Knutz's spacesuit on the left exactly?

A.

B.

C.

D.

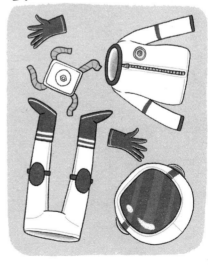

Answer on p239

CHAPTER FIVE:
Lost in Space

Boltz grabbed my hand.

"We might be floating in space," she said. "But at least we won't float away from each other."

I glanced back the way we'd come. Earth was a pale blue circle, and the space station would still be orbiting around it somewhere, too small for us to see.

My heart **raced** and I found myself taking quick breaths. I worried this would use up my remaining oxygen faster, so I forced myself to breathe slowly in and out.

"I hope the people and animals back on Earth find out about what we did," I said.

"I'm sure Venus and Mars will tell everyone the **truth**," said Boltz. "No matter how much Brandon tries to hide it."

I turned to the deep blackness of space ahead of us.

"I wonder why he wanted all the plans to fail?" I asked. "Why would anyone want Earth to be destroyed?"

"Who knows?" asked Boltz. "Maybe too much time in space drove him mad. I don't suppose we'll ever find out."

I wondered what Brandon would say when Venus and Mars returned to the station and confronted him. I wished I could be there to see it.

"How must he have felt when we actually managed to knock the asteroid off course?" I asked. "His **fiendish plan** was foiled after all."

"He probably had to pretend to be pleased," said Boltz.

I looked back at Earth. Weakness spread through my limbs as I remembered how helpless and **remote** we were.

A star in the distance caught my attention. It seemed to be getting larger.

"What do you think that is?" I asked, pointing at it.

"Probably nothing," said Boltz. "I want it to be a spacecraft that's been sent out to rescue us, but there's no way it can be."

She unclipped her telescope from her belt.

"No harm in taking a look, though," she said.

Telescopes focus light so you can see distant objects more clearly. There are two main types:

1. Refractor telescopes use glass lenses with a special angled lens called a 'star diagonal'. Thanks to the star diagonal, images appear the right way up when you look through most refractor telescopes.

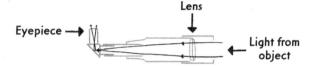

2. Reflector telescopes use mirrors. The images appear upside down when you look through most reflector telescopes.

My telescope is a refractor telescope. All of these images have been taken with a refractor telescope apart from one. Can you spot the image that has been taken with a reflector telescope?

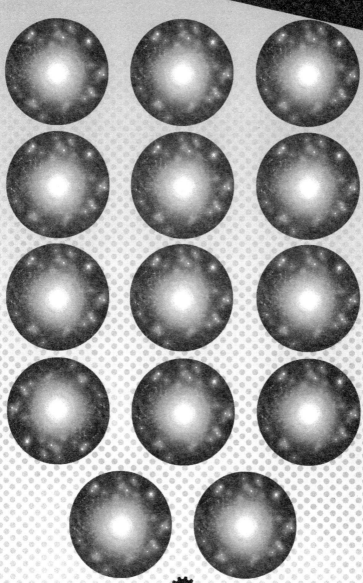

Answer on p240

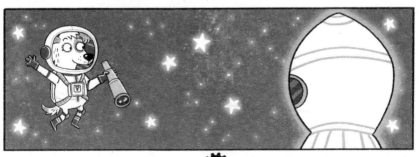

There were only two seats in the spacecraft, but we grabbed the backs of them and **clung on**.

"You saved our lives," I said.

"And you two saved the lives of everyone on Earth with your quick thinking," said Venus.

Mars pushed the joystick forwards and the craft picked up speed. We gripped the seats even tighter.

"We almost didn't make it to you," he said. "Brandon was steering us back to the station, and I struggled to override his control."

"In the end, we had to shut down the entire spacecraft," said Venus. "For all we knew, it might never have restarted. But we managed to get it going again, and this time we could steer it."

Boltz leant forwards and patted Mars on the shoulder.

"Thanks for coming back for us. You'll never be forgotten for rescuing the world's greatest animal inventor."

Mars let go of the joystick and turned around.

"Excuse me. I'M the world's greatest animal inventor. Look at my solar-powered mouse-catching machine if you don't believe me. It has a 95% success rate, except in cloudy weather."

The craft lurched violently to the side, and Venus had to grab the controls.

"There'll be plenty of time to discuss that when we're back on Earth," she said. "But first we need to get back to the station and confront Brandon."

"We'll need to find some **solid evidence** that he's guilty," said Mars. "At the moment, it's our word against his."

Earth was looming larger ahead of us.

"You two keep him distracted and we'll explore," said Boltz. "There's bound to be something that proves what he's been up to."

"Do you have any idea why he wanted the asteroid to hit Earth?" I asked. "I can't understand how anyone could possibly benefit from that."

Venus shrugged.

"Not really," she said. "We intercepted a signal he sent back to Earth, but I don't know what it means."

The signal was some sort of coded mathematical message. I jotted it down.

I think the answer to each of these calculations matches a letter in the alphabet.

If you work out the answers and match them to the letters on the right, it might reveal a hidden message.

14 ÷ 2   3 x 5

4 x 5   22 -7

25 - 6   4 x 4   1346 – 1345
9 ÷ 3   2 + 3

2 x 4   9 + 6   5 x 4
25 ÷ 5   3 x 4

Can you use Venus' code to uncover the message on the previous page?

A = 1   N = 14
B = 2   O = 15
C = 3   P = 16
D = 4   Q = 17
E = 5   R = 18
F = 6   S = 19
G = 7   T = 20
H = 8   U = 21
I = 9   V = 22
J = 10   W = 23
K = 11   X = 24
L = 12   Y = 25
M = 13   Z = 26

We sneaked down the corridor to the sleeping pods. They were three identical booths with sleeping bags, but no pillows or mattresses. It made them look pretty uncomfortable, even though I knew you didn't need anything to rest against when you were in freefall.

There was a **Velcro folder** attached to the wall of each pod, and all three astronauts had tucked their space-centre lanyards inside. Brandon's was in the pod in the middle, and Boltz took it out.

"This says it was issued two years ago," she said. "Yet it looks new, as though it's hardly been used at all."

She tucked it into the pocket of her spacesuit.

I reached into the folder and pulled out a wad of paper. There were pictures of asteroids, as well as diagrams of the drones in different formations.

"Any clues?" asked Boltz.

"Not really," I said. "He did a lot of planning for the drone attack, but I can't see any clues that he wanted to **sabotage** it."

Boltz pulled herself out of the booth and glanced down the corridor.

"Keep looking," she said. "But make it quick. If he's really hidden something in here, he'll come after us soon."

I tried to leaf through the papers faster, but accidentally let go of them. They floated around the pod.

"Whoops!" I said.

Boltz came back in and we flapped around frantically, snatching the papers.

I spotted her grabbing a **photograph** of someone and shoving it into her pocket, but I couldn't make out who it was.

As we were tucking the last sheets of paper back in, I noticed a **bar chart**. The writing on it was clear, but I couldn't work out what it had to do with anything.

Graphs are used to show the relationship between pieces of data. Most graphs have two axes, which represent numbers or variables. An x-axis is the horizontal line, and the y-axis is the vertical line.

A bar chart is a graph that plots things using bars – the bigger the bar, the more of that thing there is. For example, this bar chart shows the types of dog biscuit that Boltz eats over a 12-day period. From this graph, we can see that her favourite flavour is chicken:

SPACE HOTEL TICKETS

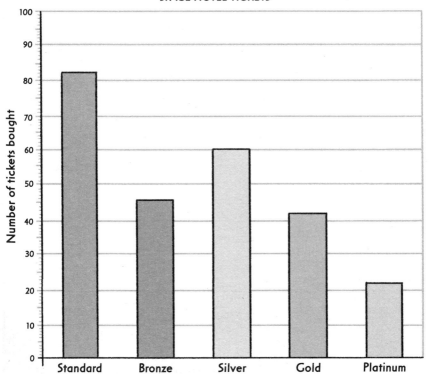

TYPE OF TICKET

Using Brandon's bar chart, can you answer the following questions?

1. How many passengers bought the most popular type of ticket?

2. How many more passengers bought bronze tickets than platinum ones?

3. Which two types of ticket can you add together to equal the amount of standard tickets?

Answer on p242

Brandon rattled the handle and pushed against the other side of the door, but Boltz held it firm.

"We saw the fuel pumps you took from the missiles. And we know you steered Venus and Mars the wrong way as they fired the missile. Why did you do it?"

The handle fell still. I could hear Brandon inside the pod, calming his breathing down.

"Those are old fuel pumps from a previous mission," he said. "Nothing to do with this one."

They looked **identical** to me. And I'd watched the 3D printer create two of them, so I knew them well.

"And I didn't do anything to change the course of Venus and Mars's craft," Brandon said. "They just missed, and they're trying to cover up for it. I'm surprised you trust them. They don't even like you."

I thought back to how rude Venus and Mars had been when we first boarded the station. For a moment, I wondered if Brandon was actually telling the truth, but then I realized it was just a trick. I was sure the bar chart proved he was **guilty**, too, but I couldn't quite work out why.

"They liked us enough to alert us about you," said Boltz. "Without them, we could never have saved Earth."

"You would," said Brandon. "Because you wouldn't have missed. We should have picked you two to go first, I realize that now. You're much better astronauts than they are."

This time I didn't let Brandon get to me. I ignored his attempt at **flattery**.

"What you're accusing me of makes no sense, anyway. Why would I want Earth to be destroyed?"

Boltz took out the photo she'd swiped earlier. It showed **Brad Piper**, the owner of the space hotels.

"This might explain it," she said.

Study this photo of Brad Piper carefully. Which of the close-ups on the opposite page match the picture exactly, and which don't?

A.

B.

C.

D.

E.

F.

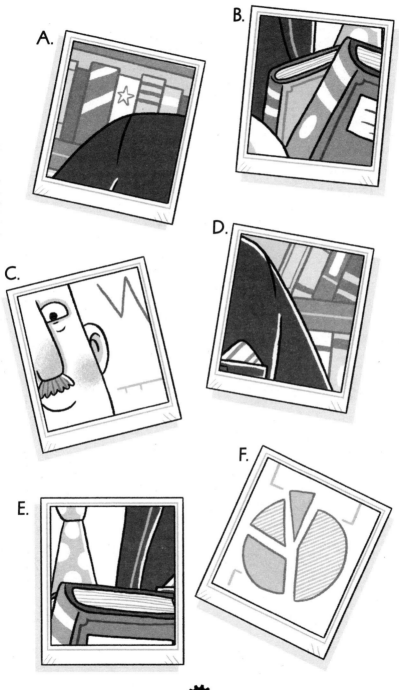

Answer on p242

He's getting away!

Brad shot down the corridor, and we sped after him. He was used to propelling himself around the station and soon got away from us.

When we reached a part of the station that split into three, Brad was out of sight. We had the option of going left, right or straight ahead.

There were signs reading '**Laboratory**' in English, Mandarin and Hindi.

We'd reached the labs belonging to the American, Chinese and Indian space agencies. These were the most important parts of the station under normal circumstances. Scientists would come up here to carry out **experiments** and find out more about space. It was only the asteroid that had halted everything.

We carried straight on into the Indian team's lab, gliding past rows of torches, microscopes, gloves, plastic tubes and pipettes.

I pulled myself up and down, gazing into every corner to see if Brad was silently waiting to pounce on us.

There was no sign of him, and I spun around so much that I got **dizzy** and had to close my eyes. Then I remembered that we were circling around Earth too, and it made me feel even dizzier.

I opened my eyes and saw Boltz sniffing a patch of what was either the ceiling or floor. She was usually great at tracking scents, but she was stuck on one spot now.

"I don't think my sense of smell works as well in space," she said. "I can't tell if he's been here or not. Let's try the other labs."

We pulled ourselves back to the point where the corridor split.

I looked right to the American lab and left to the Chinese one.

"Which should we try?" I asked.

"Let's pick the longest one," said Boltz. "There will be more places for him to hide."

The American and the Chinese teams have measured their labs using two different systems. The American team have used the imperial system, which measures things in feet, and the Chinese team have used the metric system, which measures things in metres.

The Chinese lab is 12 metres long.

The American lab is 41 feet long.

1 metre is roughly 3.3 feet.

Using this information, can you work out which lab is the longest?

Once you have an answer, find your way through the maze of corridors on the page opposite to get to the lab you think is the longest.

Chinese
Laboratory

American
Laboratory

Answer on p243

We entered the lab ...

171

Brad forced a thick metal door down on top of us. I heard a lock **click** into place.

"That's strange," I said. "Why does this sleeping pod have a lock on the outside?"

"If this is a sleeping pod, it belongs to someone very untidy," said Boltz.

I looked around. There were empty food packets drifting about, as well as T-shirts, vests, socks and underpants.

Boltz pointed to a sweat stain on one of the socks.

"Yuk! I'm glad my sense of smell isn't working now," she said. "This looks like dirty laundry."

I thought about the drops of water that had floated around earlier, and wondered how you could wash clothes in freefall.

"How do they even do laundry here?" I asked.

"They don't," said Boltz. "There isn't enough water. They just wear them until they're dirty and then put them in the **trash chute**."

She stopped, and her eyes widened.

"Wait a minute," she said. "That's where we are. THIS is the trash chute!"

She banged her paws on the door.

"Let us out!" she cried.

"Never!" came Brad's voice from the other side. "That asteroid was going to mean a fresh start for humankind, and you two ruined it."

I glanced down at the round door at the far end of the chute.

"What happens if we get **trapped** here?" I asked. "Do we have to wait for a cargo ship to come and pick up the trash?"

"The trash isn't picked up by a cargo ship," said Boltz. "It's ejected into space and burns up when it re-enters the Earth's atmosphere."

I gulped, and pulled myself up to the door.

"Open up!" I yelled.

Brad just laughed from the other side.

"Hey, look at this," said Boltz.

There was a small keypad next to the lock with '**Emergency release**' written next to it. Someone had scrawled letters and numbers on the wall near it.

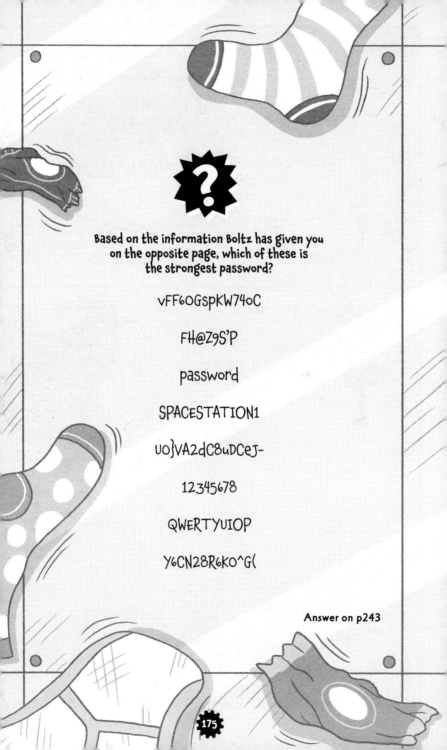

Based on the information Boltz has given you on the opposite page, which of these is the strongest password?

vFF6OGspKW74oC

FH@Z9S'P

password

SPACESTATION1

UO}VA2dC8uDCeJ-

12345678

QWERTYUIOP

Y6CN28R6KO^G(

Answer on p243

175

The door clicked open.

CHAPTER SIX:
Brought to Justice

Mei and Amir dragged Brad back to the control room, where Venus and Mars were holding short lengths of electrical cable. They tied them around his wrists and ankles, and fixed him to a handrail.

"Why did you do it, Brandon?" asked Amir.

He stared back in silence.

"That isn't Brandon," I said. "That's **Brad Piper**, the owner of the four space hotels. We found a photograph and a bar graph in his sleeping pod."

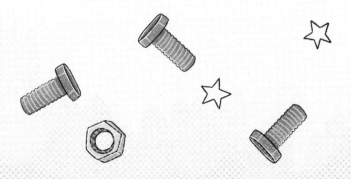

Mei gasped.

"I should have known something was wrong," she said. "But I was so distracted by the asteroid, I wasn't thinking straight."

"I blame myself," said Amir, shaking his head. "I thought it was strange that the American team sent an astronaut I'd never even met before. I should have checked things with them."

Brad **writhed** around, trying to pull the cables loose, but they held fast.

"We should have been more suspicious, too," said Venus. "We were so focused on competing, we didn't pay enough attention to him."

"The only person to blame for any of this is Brad. He created a fake identity to get to this station, he hacked the programming of the drones so they wouldn't work and he sabotaged both attempts to fire a missile at the asteroid."

Boltz took the lanyard out of her pocket and handed it to Mei.

"We found this in his sleeping pod," she said. "It says it was issued two years ago, but it looks **brand new**."

Mei examined it and shook her head.

"I really should have picked up on that. And I should have known from the check digits that something was wrong. I'm usually so careful about everything, too."

Barcodes are tiny rectangles made of lines that represent the digits from 0 to 9. They appear on everything from supermarket products and entertainment tickets to ID badges. Machines scan them to generate a long series of numbers very quickly.

Barcodes have 'check digits' to make sure they've been scanned properly.

Check digits are calculated using algorithms. In our algorithm, the check digit is calculated the following way:

Add the first 12 digits together.
The check digit is the difference between the sum of the first 12 digits and the closest multiple of 10 to this sum.

For example:

912444569121 **2**

The sum of 9+1+2+4+4+4+5+6+9+1+2+1 is 48. The closest multiple of 10 to this is 50. 50 - 48 = 2, so the check digit is 2.

I should have known Brad's pass was fake, because the check digits of his barcode are wrong.

Can you work out which of these is Brad's barcode, using the information on the left-hand page?

A.

787492086834 4

B.

622629530521 7

C.

558282011362 3

D.

684424619334 4

Answer on p244

The rest of you wait here. The World Space Agency is sending up another craft for you.

Brad flipped around violently as Mei and Amir dragged him away.

"You ruined everything," he cried. "The world would have been so much better if I'd had my way."

"Life would have been wiped out!" I said. "In what way would it have been better?"

Brad fell still and fixed his eyes on me.

"It wouldn't have been wiped out," he said. "Over 250 people are in my **space hotels** right now. They're waiting out the impact of an asteroid that will never come. They would have started the world again. It would have been a second chance for humanity. There would have been no countries, no borders and no wars."

Boltz jabbed her finger at him.

"And who would have been in charge of this new world?" she asked. "Let me guess — you."

Brad nodded.

"Of course," he said. "I'm a successful businessman, after all. And I'd have made a great leader. Better than any of those clowns who've ruled in the past. I would have been the first truly just and fair leader."

"Fair?" cried Venus. "Just? You were prepared to let billions die for your **stupid plan**."

Brad shook his head.

"The asteroid was our great opportunity to reset," he said. "There are eight billion people in the world. That's doubled in my lifetime. And that's not to mention hundreds of millions of cats and dogs. The world is too crowded."

"Yes, the world's population is growing," I said. "But we can make things better for everyone through **science** and **technology**. All humans and animals have the right to share the world, and no one gets to decide who lives and who dies."

Amir and Mei pulled Brad down the corridor towards the docking bay.

"We'd better get back," said Mei. "We don't want to keep the police waiting."

Here is a graph of the world's human population over time. Brad said that the population has doubled since he was born.

1. Using that information, can you work out which year he was born in?

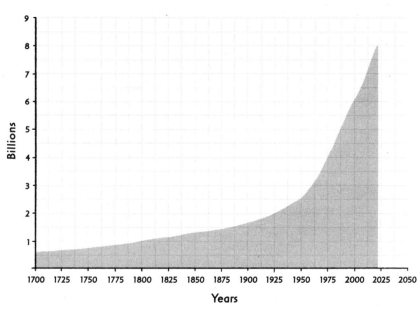

And here is a graph showing the population of dogs and cats over 140 years. Can you answer the following questions about it?

2. How many cats were there in the world in 1940, according to this graph?

3. How many dogs were there in the world in 1965, according to this graph?

4. In what year were the populations of dogs and cats the same?

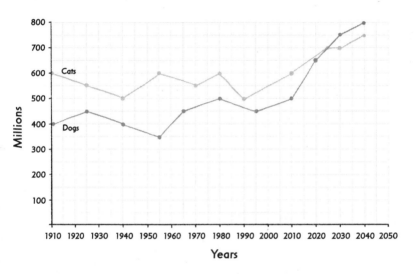

Answer on p244

Brad looks angry. What if he manages to hit the controls?

Don't worry. The landing module is detaching. There's nothing he can do now.

Soon after Mei, Amir and Brad had splashed down, a spacecraft with 'WSA 003' on the side docked in the bay of the space station.

An American woman stepped out. She took her helmet off and her long red hair floated into a halo around her head.

"Let me shake the hands and paws of the heroes who **saved the planet**," she said.

She grabbed us one by one and shook us so forcefully that we bobbed up and down.

"Everyone knows all about you on Earth," she said. "So many people and animals want to meet you."

"Great," I said.

I tried to sound excited, but the truth was that I'd rather have gone straight to bed than meet anyone new. We'd circled Earth so many times, and seen so many sunrises and sunsets, that I felt like I'd been awake for a month.

The woman held the door to the spacecraft open for us.

"You do remember how to get back to Earth, don't you?" she asked.

I knew we'd covered it in training, but my brain was so jumbled that I couldn't recall it exactly.

"Er … I think so," I said.

"Don't worry," said Mars, tapping the side of his head. "It's all in here. I'll undock us, and give the thrusters a blast. We'll drop back into Earth's atmosphere and I'll open the parachute."

The woman saluted us as we fixed our helmets on and got into the spacecraft. I took the front seat with Mars, while Boltz and Venus got in behind us.

"Excellent," said the woman. "Just be careful to get the angle of entry into the Earth's atmosphere exactly right. If you get it just slightly wrong, you could burn up, or **bounce back** into space."

Mars pointed to the controls in front of me.

"You can take care of that, can't you?" he asked.

"Of course," I said.

Returning a spacecraft to Earth is a nail-biting process!

Can you help Knutz and Mars put the images on the right in the correct order, to match the sequence below?

1. Your spacecraft detaches from the main space station and mission control sends you the data you need to return the craft to Earth. This data ensures you enter Earth's atmosphere at exactly the right speed and angle.

2. A quick blast on the spacecraft's thrusters slows it down. Then Earth's gravity pulls the craft towards it.

3. As the spacecraft approaches Earth's atmosphere, it detaches into three parts — only the part you're in, the landing module, will continue back to Earth.

4. The module begins re-entry into Earth's atmosphere. When it does this, it encounters enormous friction, which causes the module to heat up. The module's heat shield protects you.

5. At about 8.5 kilometres above Earth, the module detaches enormous parachutes to slow the craft down as it heads towards the surface.

6. You land with a splash in the ocean.

A.

B.

C.

D.

E.

F.

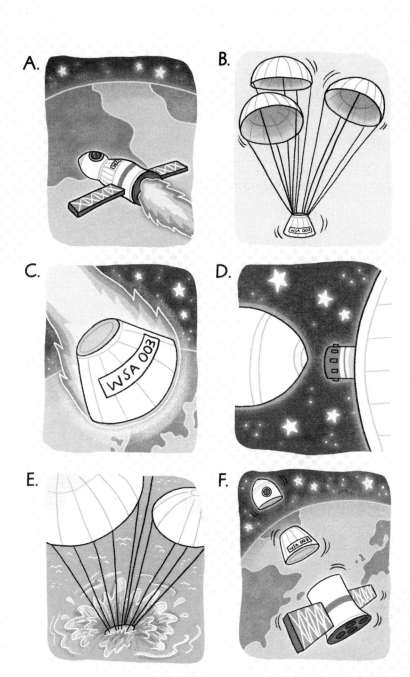

Answer on p245

As soon as we climbed up to the deck of the recovery boat, reporters **swarmed** around us and asked questions.

I was so used to being in space that at first I thought I could just float away and get some peace. Then I remembered that I was back in Earth's gravity and escape wouldn't be so easy.

A reporter shoved a microphone into my face.

"When did you first realize that Brandon wasn't who he was claiming to be?" he asked.

So much had happened that I struggled to put it all in order.

"His lanyard was too new," I said. "And he had a bar chart."

The reporter grinned, but I could see confusion in his eyes.

Behind me, I could hear Boltz, Venus and Mars impressing the other interviewers with their **heroic tales** of saving Earth.

"That's fascinating," said the reporter.

He slipped away to talk to the others.

I pushed through the crowd and found an indoor area where glasses and jugs of fruit juice were laid out on a table.

I poured myself some fresh orange juice. My senses of smell and taste were returning, and I took the time to savour the sharp, tangy flavour. I'd had to flap around the control room for my last drink, so I appreciated the simple pleasure of just being able to sip this one down.

There was a bench with a cushion on it in the corner of the room, and I wondered if I could get away with having a nap until we reached shore.

But then I heard the door swing open and turned to see a woman with a microphone and a man with a large camera barging in.

"We can now bring you an **exclusive** live interview with one of the space heroes," said the woman.

Answer on p245

I shook off the reporters and joined everyone on the top deck.

Welcome back, team. There's just one more thing we need your help with.

WE ♥ VENUS

WE ♥ BOLTZ

WORLD SPACE AGENCY

We entered **mission headquarters**, and the staff stood up and applauded us.

"You all did a great job," said Mei. "Brad's with the police right now, and it looks like he'll be going to jail for a long time."

"The only thing left for us to deal with is all the customers on his space hotels," said Amir. "They thought they'd be returning to Earth to build a new world. Instead, they'll be coming back to the old one as villains."

Amir tapped his laptop, and the inside of one of the space hotels appeared. It looked a lot like the space station, except that it had **luxury** armchairs instead of workstations.

A large group of passengers had been tied to the handrails and were looking flustered. Three World Space Agency astronauts were swooping around and guarding them.

"So, what do you think we should do with them?" asked Mei.

"Show no mercy," said Venus. "They were prepared to watch Earth get destroyed for the sake of their new society. We can't just let them go back to their lives as if nothing happened."

"Lock them up forever. If we set them free, they'll only do more bad things."

I could see what they meant. These people had been **traitors** to their fellow humans. But, on the other hand, they'd probably been talked into it by Brad. Maybe there was a way to for them to get a fresh start after all.

"I've got an idea. Why don't we bring them back here and teach them to become scientists? Then we can turn the hotels into space labs, and they can carry out useful experiments. After all, they've been trained to survive in space, and it would be a shame to waste that."

Let me see how long it would take to bring the passengers back down to Earth.

There are 63 passengers on each space hotel, plus 3 World Space Agency astronauts. Each hotel has just 1 docking bay, which means that 3 people can leave every 2 hours.

The journey to Earth, including the time it takes to get from the sea to the space centre, is 4 hours.

How long would it take to get everyone from one of the hotels back to the space centre from the time the first group left?

Answer on p245

THE END

USEFUL WORDS

3D
Three-dimensional; something that has depth and is not flat.

Airlock
A special chamber on a space station that astronauts use to enter and exit. It has one door into the space station, and one to outer space, and it keeps the air inside the space station.

Animation
A film made by playing illustrations at high speed to look like they are moving.

Asteroid
A piece of rock that orbits the Sun.

Atmosphere
A layer of gases surrounding a planet.

Atoms
Tiny particles which make up everything around us.

Axis

In maths, a reference line used to measure data on a graph or grid. On a co-ordinate grid, the horizontal axis is called the x-axis and the vertical axis is called the y-axis.

Check digit

A number that is used in a barcode to help check that the rest of the numbers are correct.

Data

A collection of facts, figures or other forms of information, which are used to analyse something or make decisions.

Drone

An aircraft that can be flown without a pilot on board.

Friction

The force of resistance that one object or surface encounters when moving over another.

Gravity

A force of attraction between all things with mass.

Hacking
Gaining access to a computer system without permission.

Landing module
The part of a spacecraft that lands on a planet or moon.

Lens
A curved piece of transparent glass or plastic which can bend light.

Multiple
In maths, a number that can be divided by other numbers. For example, 20 is a multiple of 10 and 2: it can be divided by 10 and 2.

Orbit
To follow a path around a planet, star or moon.

Population
The number of people or animals living in a particular area.

Program
A set of instructions that tells a computer exactly what to do.

Solar array
A group of connected solar panels.

Solar panel
Devices which capture sunlight and turn it into energy.

Sum
The result of adding two or more numbers together.

Thrust
The force created by an engine that moves a rocket forwards.

BONUS GAME ONE

Rockets are made up of different sections, called 'stages'. Can you work out which set below contains all of the stages that make up this rocket exactly?

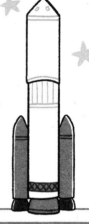

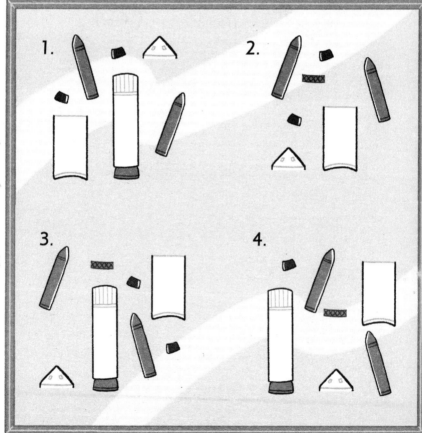

BONUS GAME TWO

Can you solve these weight-based puzzles?

Tortilla
70g

Cracker
10g

Dog biscuit
5g

Apple
15g

Chicken
60g

Spinach
8g

Cookie
20g

BONUS GAME THREE

Can you answer the following co-ordinate questions? Study the map to find the answer. Remember, the first number tells you where on the horizontal axis it is, and the second tells you where it is on the vertical axis.

1. What can you find at (G,4)?

2. How many rocks are at (M,3)?

3. What are the co-ordinates of the three small spiral galaxies?

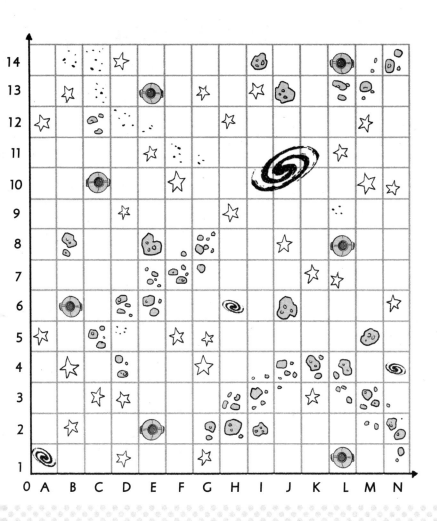

BONUS GAME FOUR

All of these drones look the same, but one is slightly different from the rest. Can you spot it?

BONUS GAME FIVE

Can you work out what the following sequences are and what's missing from each one?

1. ▲ ▲ ▲ ▲ ▲ ? ▲ ▲ ▲

2. ▲ ▲ ▲ ? ▲ ▲ ▲ ▲ ▲ ▲ ▲ ▲

3. ▲ ▲ ▲ ▲ ▲ ? ▲ ▲ ▲ ▲

4. ▲ ▲ ▲ ? ▲ ▲ ▲ ▲ ▲ ▲ ▲

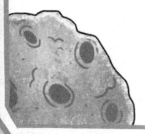

BONUS GAME SIX

Can you use your knowledge of the solar system to work out which of the words from the list below will complete these facts?

Mercury is _____ than all the other planets.

Saturn and _____ have rings.

Earth is _____ than Mars.

There are _____ planets in our solar system.

The _____ is at the centre of our solar system.

Missing words:
Sun
Uranus
larger
smaller
eight

BONUS GAME SEVEN

Study this bar chart, which shows the number of toys purchased by 100 dogs in the course of a year. Then answer the questions below.

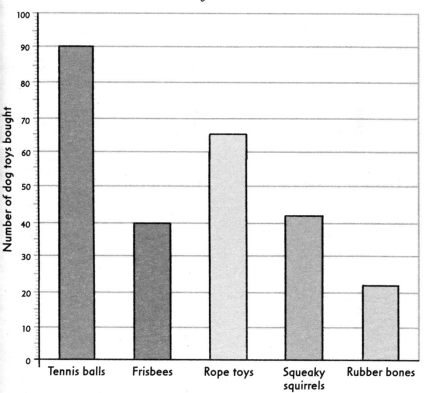

1. How many dogs bought tennis balls?

2. How many dogs bought rope toys?

3. How many more dogs bought Frisbees than rubber bones?

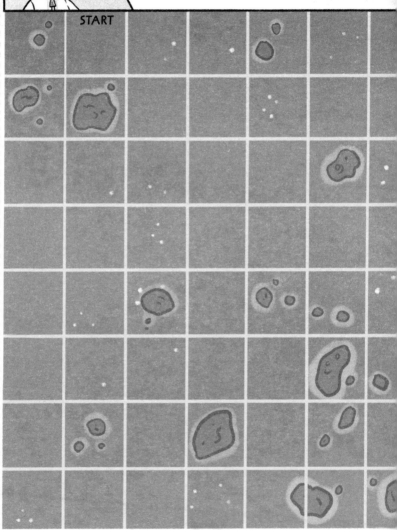

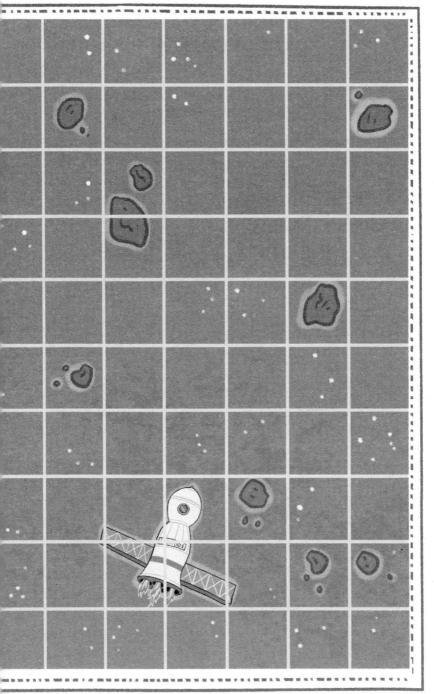

BONUS GAME NINE

Can you solve the following sums to find out
some fun, real-life stats about space?

$2 \times 8 =$ **The number of sunrises
and sunsets the crew of the
International Space Station
see each day!**

$27 - 15 =$ **The number of people
who have walked on the Moon.**

$100 \div 100 =$ **The number of
spacecraft that have
explored Neptune up close.**

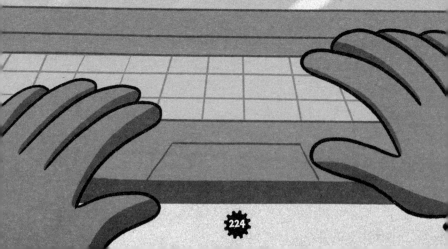

BONUS GAME TEN

Can you find the following groups of planets in the grid?

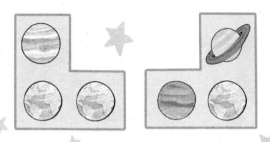 

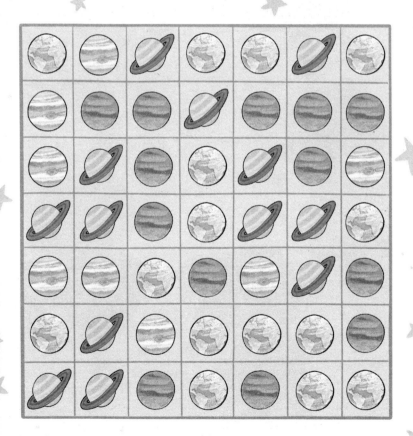

BONUS GAME ELEVEN

Which of these silhouettes matches the picture exactly?

BONUS GAME TWELVE

Which of the water pouches below contain prime numbers?

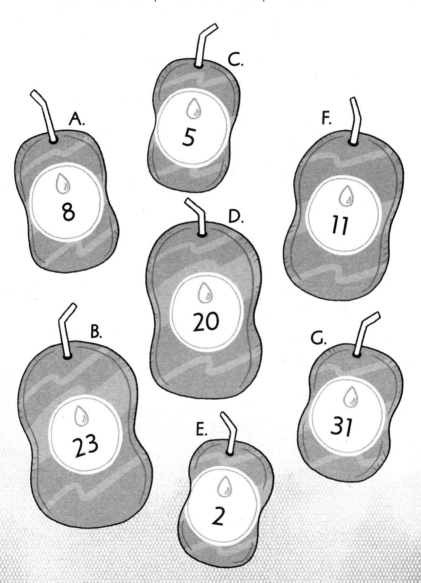

ANSWERS:
CHAPTER ONE

Pages 14–15

The stages and images go in the following order:
First: C
Second: E
Third: A
Fourth: D
Fifth: B

They match the following images:
C = 3, E = 1, A = 5, D = 2, B = 4

Pages 18–19

Boltz will have to press the black button 10 times.

Pages 26–27

1. The space station goes around Earth 8 times in 12 hours.
2. The space station goes around Earth 16 times in 24 hours.

Pages 30–31

1. Two in three, or roughly 67%
2. 6%

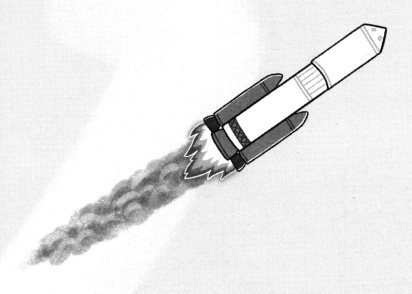

ANSWERS:
CHAPTER TWO

Pages 36–37

The other six drones are located in: (B,6), (C,10), (E,2), (E,13), (L,1) and (L,8)

Pages 42–43

Pages 48–49

7 x 3 = 21, so combined the astronauts will need 21 litres of water per day.

To reach that total with the fewest number of pouches, you need to pick 13L and 8L.

Pages 54–55

Boltz = 72g (5g + 5g + 50g + 12g)
Mars = 82g (4g + 4g + 4g + 60g + 10g)
Knutz = 95g (20g + 50g + 15g + 10g)
Venus = 100g (60g + 12g + 20g + 8g)
Mei = 93g (60g + 8g + 10g + 15g)
Amir = 145g (70g + 60g + 15g)
Brandon = 105g (50g + 10g + 10g + 15g + 20g)

Amir's meal weighs the most.

Pages 60–61

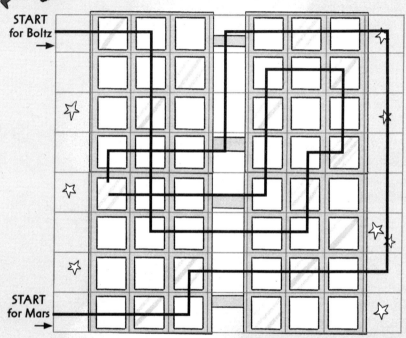

START for Boltz →

START for Mars →

Pages 66–67

1. 19:00, or 7 o'clock in the evening
2. 21:00, or 9 o'clock in the evening
3. 05:00, or 5 o'clock in the morning

ANSWERS:
CHAPTER THREE

Pages 74–75

Route B.

Pages 80–81

The third line of code has been altered. The laser needs to fire for a period of time in order to work.

Pages 86–87

Model C matches the missing fuel pump exactly.

Pages 92–93

The other prime numbers are: 5, 7, 11, 13, 17 and 19.

236

Pages 100–101

Height: Click on button '2 x'. 25 cm x 2 = 50 cm
Depth: Click on button '2.5 x'. 20 cm x 2.5 = 50 cm
Length: Click on button '1.5 x'. 50 cm x 1.5 = 75 cm

Pages 106–107

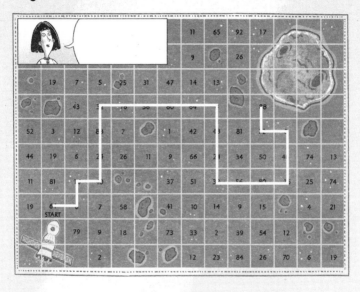

Pages 110–111

111 − 31 = 80

The answers to the other sums are:

9 x 8 = 72	53 + 26 = 79
170 ÷ 2 = 85	4 x 13 = 52
8 + 62 = 70	10 x 7 = 70
8 x 12 = 96	120 − 45 = 75
16 + 63 = 79	

ANSWERS:
CHAPTER FOUR

Pages 118–119

A2 B4 C1 D3

Pages 124–125

Knutz and Boltz need to use frame F.

Pages 130–131

Pages 138–139

Set B matches Knutz's spacesuit exactly.

ANSWERS:
CHAPTER FIVE

Pages 144–145

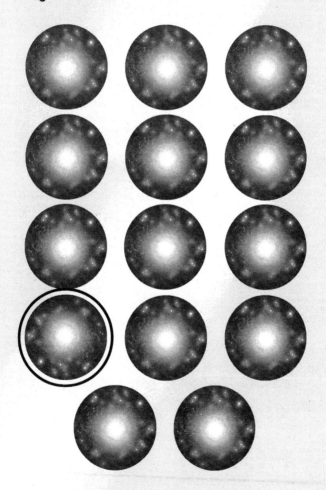

Pages 150–151

The code says: GO TO SPACE HOTEL

$14 \div 2 = 7$ (G)
$3 \times 5 = 15$ (O)

$4 \times 5 = 20$ (T)
$22 - 7 = 15$ (O)

$25 - 6 = 19$ (S)
$4 \times 4 = 16$ (P)
$1346 - 1345 = 1$ (A)
$9 \div 3 = 3$ (C)
$2 + 3 = 5$ (E)

$2 \times 4 = 8$ (H)
$9 + 6 = 15$ (O)
$5 \times 4 = 20$ (T)
$25 \div 5 = 5$ (E)
$3 \times 4 = 12$ (L)

GO TO
SPACE
HOTEL

Pages 156–157

1. 82
2. 24
3. Silver and Platinum

Pages 162–163

D and E don't match exactly the main image exactly.

Pages 168–169

The American Lab is the longest
(12 x 3.3 feet = 39.6 feet, so the Chinese Lab
is shorter than the American Lab).

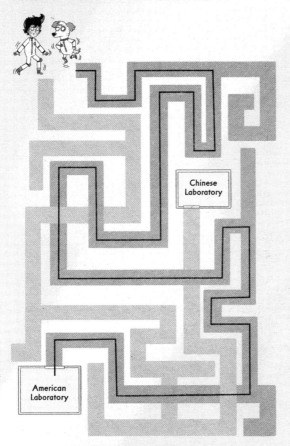

Pages 174–175

The strongest password is: U0}VA2dC8uDCeJ-
It contains no recognizable words and a mix of
uppercase letters, lowercase letters, numbers and
symbols.

ANSWERS:
CHAPTER SIX

Pages 182–183

The incorrect barcode is B. 622629530521 7
6 + 2 + 2 + 6 + 2 + 9 + 5 + 3 + 0 + 5 + 2 + 1 =
43. The nearest multiple of 10 is 40. 43 - 40 = 3, so
the check digit should be 3.

Pages 188–189

1. 1975
2. 500 million
3. 450 million
4. 2025

Pages 194–195

1 = D
2 = A
3 = F
4 = C
5 = B
6 = E

Pages 200–201

1. Freefall
2. H_2O
3. Equilateral
4. One
5. Mercury, Venus, Earth, Mars, Jupiter, Saturn, Uranus, Neptune
6. True

Pages 206–207

They could all be back in 46 hours, as the last group would leave after 42 hours, and it would take four hours for them to return to the Space Centre.

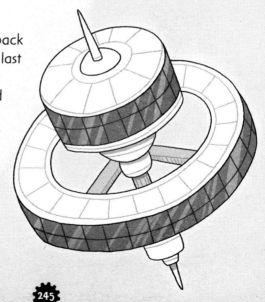

ANSWERS:
BONUS GAMES

Page 214

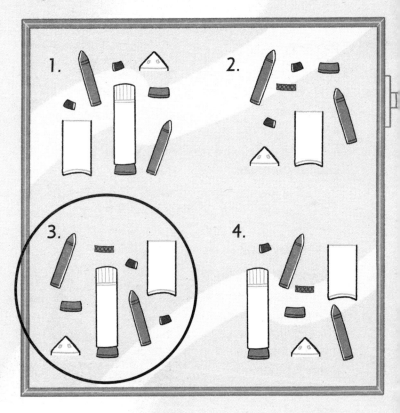

Page 215

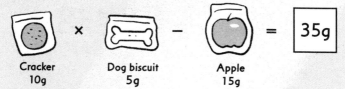

Cracker
10g

Dog biscuit
5g

Apple
15g

= 35g

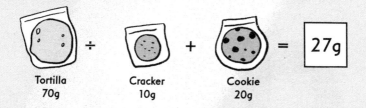

Tortilla
70g

Cracker
10g

Cookie
20g

= 27g

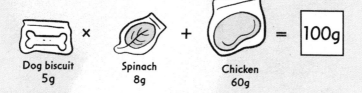

Dog biscuit
5g

Spinach
8g

Chicken
60g

= 100g

Pages 216–217

1. A star
2. Four rocks
3. (A,1), (H,6) and (N,4)

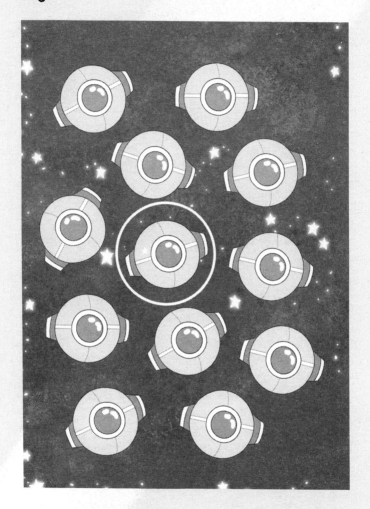

1.

2.

3.

4.

Page 220

Mercury is smaller than all the other planets.

Saturn and Uranus have rings.

Earth is larger than Mars.

There are eight planets in our solar system.

The Sun is at the centre of our solar system.

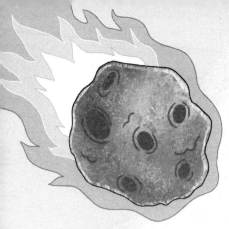

Page 221

1. 90
2. 65
3. 18

Pages 222–223

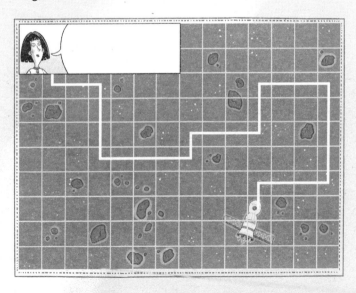

$2 \times 8 = 16$

$27 - 15 = 12$

$100 \div 100 = 1$

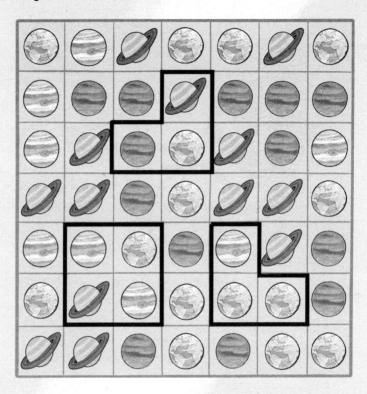

Page 226

C.

Page 227

B, C, F, E and G

Pages 228–229

1. 35%
2. Mission Elapsed time, or MET
3. Computer-aided design
4. False. The bottom number is called the denominator. The top number is called the numerator.
5. Mirrors
6. 1 foot